OUR SOULS,

THEY ARE NOT DEAD!

Poems, Prayers, and Promises

for the

Poor Souls in Purgatory

by

Donna Sue Berry

Edited by
Eugenia L. Zanone
Jane Frances Privett

Berry Books Publishing

Eternal rest grant unto them, O Lord;
and let perpetual light shine upon them.
May they rest in peace. Amen.

ISBN 978-0-692-96816-1

Dedicated

to the

Poor Souls in Purgatory

Those We Loved

and

Those We Never Knew

St. Gertrude

Prayer to Release Poor Souls from Purgatory According to St. Gertrude the Great

Eternal Father,
I offer You the Most Precious Blood
of Thy Divine Son, Jesus,
in union with the Masses said
throughout the world today,
for all the Holy Souls in purgatory,
for sinners everywhere,
for sinners in the universal Church,
for those in my own home,
and within my family.
Amen.

Ways to Help the Poor Souls in Purgatory

Make a very fervent 'Sign of the Cross' while remembering the Poor Souls.

When attending Mass, offer it up for them.

Sprinkle Holy Water and ask God to let it touch the Poor Souls.

Light a candle for them at church.

Say a Rosary for the Poor Souls.

Offer up your suffering as penance for the Poor Souls.

Pray short indulgenced prayers for them.

Indulgenced Prayer

May the most just, most high, most adorable will of God be done in all things, and praised and magnified forever.

(From the Raccolta)

Table of Contents

Our Souls, They are Not Dead! - 1

I Have Been Here for a Long Time - 4

A Cemetery in Montana - 11

Prayers for the Dying, Prayers for the Dead - 13

When They Come to Me - 15

Purgatory and Roadside Crosses - 16

Traditional Catholic Prayers -24

Then they all blessed the just judgment of the Lord, who had discovered the things that were hidden.

And so, betaking themselves to prayers, they besought him, that the sin which had been committed might be forgotten. But the most valiant Judas exhorted the people to keep themselves from sin, forasmuch as they saw before their eyes what had happened, because of the sins of those that were slain.

And making a gathering, he sent twelve thousand drachms of silver to Jerusalem for sacrifice to be offered for the sins of the dead, thinking well and religiously for sacrifice concerning the resurrection (For if he had not hoped that they that were slain should rise again, it would have seemed superfluous and vain to pray for the dead). And because he considered that they who had fallen asleep with godliness, had great grace laid up for them.

It is therefore a holy and wholesome thought to pray for the dead, that they may be loosed from sins *(Douay-Rheims, 2 Machabees 12:41 – 46).*

Our Souls, They Are Not Dead!

In silence late one evening, I found myself alone,
Enjoying for the moment some peacefulness at home.
A steamy cup of coffee with a shot of Irish cream,
Had lulled me into comfort as I drifted off to dream.
The mistiness around me draped my shoulders like a shawl,
While voices so familiar seemed to beckon with a call.

“Pray for us, please pray for us, and offer up your pain.
We need your acts of charity to fall on us like rain.
Please sprinkle holy water, light a candle in our stead,
For we long to see our Savior, our souls, they are not dead!”

Stunned, I peered in silence as I strained to hear each sound,
From the shadows there before me, as I knelt on holy ground.
Daddy? No, my grandpa? Was that my late but dearest aunt?
Did I hear the voice of family in their soft and pleading chant?

“Pray for us, please pray for us, and offer up your pain,
We need your acts of charity to fall on us like rain.
Please sprinkle holy water, light a candle in our stead,
For we long to see our Savior, our souls, they are not dead!”

Their entreaty begged compassion, with a plea for so
much prayer,
That I quickly sought the face of God to ask Him then
and there,
"For the Souls in Purgatory, dear Father, grant release,
So soon their cries are silenced when at last they dwell in peace.
Still if my dad therein resides or my grandpa and my aunt,
Please take them soon to heaven, of this I ask you grant."

That is when I made the promise, to pray and not forget,
My family who may need me still to help repay their debt.
Their voices slowly faded, I could barely hear their call.
Quiet darkness overtook me, and I began to fall.
Then with a start I jumped in pain, hot coffee on my pants,
But still it seemed, I heard the sound of Poor Souls as they chant.

"Pray for us, please pray for us, and offer up your pain.
We need your acts of charity to fall on us like rain.
Please sprinkle holy water, light a candle in our stead,
For we long to see our Savior; our souls, they are not dead."

Merciful Lord Jesus, grant them everlasting rest.

Pie Iesu Domine, dona eis requeiem simpiternam.

(From the Raccolta)

Eternal Father, by virtue of Thine generosity and love, I ask that Thou accept all my actions, and that Thou dost multiply their value in favor of every soul in Purgatory. Through Christ our Lord. Amen.

"Let us help and commemorate them. If Job's sons were purified by their father's sacrifice [Job 1:5], why would we doubt that our offerings for the dead bring them some consolation? Let us not hesitate to help those who have died and to offer our prayers for them." - St. John Chrysostom.

I Have Been Here for a Long Time

I have been here for a long time,
As you can surely see.
All friends and family dead and gone,
None left to pray for me.
If only I had known in life,
What waited past death's door,
I would have sacrificed and prayed,
More than I had before.
I did just what I had to do,
At least that's what I thought.
But now I see that I fell short,
From what the Church had taught.
These purgatory pains are real,
The Father's gift of grace,
A time to cleanse myself from sin,
So, I can see God's Face.
My contrition was imperfect,
My heart and will so frail,
Without these cleansing holy fires,
I would end up in hell.
And if by chance you read these words,
Please say a prayer for me,
That soon my soul is spotless and
The Father's face I see.

Why are they called "The Poor Souls"?

They are called the *Poor Souls in Purgatory* for a reason. It is because they are the souls of people who have died in a state of grace, but who are not able to enter heaven yet because they owe a debt of temporal punishment due for their sins which have been forgiven. The Poor Souls cannot pray, offer sacrifice, or give suffrages for themselves. There is nothing that they can do to merit any relief from the pains that they experience in purgatory. They are called the Church Suffering, and they covet the Holy Sacrifice of the Mass, our prayers, fasting, sacrifices, and almsgiving in atonement to help relieve their pain. Holy Mother Church exhorts us that when we offer our sufferings, united with the Passion of Christ, and apply it to the Poor Souls, that it may cause their relief or release and entrance into heaven.

Under the Usual Conditions . . .

How many times have you heard, "*You may gain a plenary indulgence under the usual conditions*?"

But what is an 'indulgence'?

According to the Catechism of the Catholic Church, "An *indulgence* is "the remission before God of the temporal punishment due for sins whose guilt has already been forgiven, which the faithful Christian, who is duly disposed, gains under certain prescribed conditions through the action of the Church which, as the minister of redemption, dispenses and applies with authority the treasury of the satisfactions of Christ and the saints.

There are two types of indulgences: plenary and partial.

1. A plenary indulgence frees a soul from ***all*** of the temporal punishment due to its sins.

2. A partial indulgence frees a soul from ***some*** of the temporal punishment due to its sins.

But what is *temporal punishment due to sins?* Temporal punishment is a 'penalty imposed' on us, either on earth or in Purgatory, where we must satisfy a debt that we owe to God for our sins.

A catechism teacher once gave a simplistic example of forgiveness with temporal punishment due. An older boy was told by his father to not throw a baseball toward the house, but the boy did it anyway and broke a window out. When the boy showed how sorry he was and apologized - the father forgave him for disobeying and for breaking the window. However, the father then imposed a penalty on him. The child would have to pay for the repair of the window.

Likewise, to gain a plenary indulgence, certain conditions are required. Those conditions are what is necessary for the 'under the usual conditions' part. The conditions to gain a plenary indulgence are:

1. **You must be in a state of grace,** meaning you must receive the sacrament of confession within twenty days of the work (several plenary indulgences may be earned per one saramental confession).

2. **Receive Eucharistic communion** (one plenary indulgence may be earned per reception of the Eucharist)

3. **Pray for the pope's intentions** (an Our Father, Hail Mary, Glory Be or other appropriate prayer)

4. **Have NO attachment to sin** (not even venial). In other words, make a complete act of your will to be attached to no sin for the intention of gaining the indulgence.

5. **Do the work.** You could use any one of these four works;

   a. Adoring the Blessed Sacrament for at least thirty minutes.
   b. Devoutly reading Sacred Scripture for at least thirty minutes.
   c. Devoutly performing the Stations of the Cross.
   d. Reciting the Rosary with members of the family, or in a church, oratory, religious community, or pious association.

Only ONE Plenary Indulgence may be gained each day.

However, many partial indulgences may be gained throughout the day.

The Saints Say

"The fire of Purgatory is the same as the fire of Hell; the difference between them is that the fire of Purgatory is not everlasting." – St. Jean Marie Baptiste Vianney

"If only you knew with what great longing these holy souls yearn for relief from their suffering. Ingratitude has never entered Heaven." – St. Margaret Mary

"We must say many prayers for the souls of the faithful departed, for one must be so pure to enter heaven" – St. Jean Marie Baptiste Vianney

"Do as I have done. Pray, pray always for the souls of the dear departed." – St. Padre Pio

"I am the Mother of all the Poor Souls, for my prayers serve to mitigate their sufferings every single hour that they remain there(purgatory)." – Our Blessed Mother to St. Bridget

Share the Wealth
Give an Indulgence Away

If you gain a plenary indulgence, you may keep it for yourself or apply it to the dead as suffrage. However, no one gaining an indulgence may apply it to other living persons.

Do not hesitate and do not wait,
They seek release to heaven's gate.

Eternal Father,
I offer Thee the Holy Wounds of Thy Son,
and His Precious Blood,
for the conversion of sinners and for the relief
of the Poor Souls in purgatory.

Eight Days in November

The faithful who during the period of eight days from November 1st – 8th visit a cemetery in the spirit of piety and devotion and pray, even mentally, for the dead, may gain a *plenary* indulgence each of those eight days under the usual conditions. These indulgences are applicable *only* to the poor souls in purgatory. On the other days of the year this indulgence is a *partial* one.

A Cemetery in Montana

In the middle of Montana
Off a dirt road on a hill,
Stands a graveyard so forgotten,
Where the dead are sleeping still.

The ground is cracked and broken from
The heat of summer's sun,
Like the souls in Purgatory,
Whose sufferings are not done.

While they thirst there for our kindness,
They long to see God's face.
But now can't fly to heaven,
Nor leave behind that place.

With their bodies in Montana,
Their souls beseech our prayer,
For only us still living can
Relieve the pain they bear.

"Oh, Father, send a storm of grace,
Let it fall like morning dew.
Rain down on them forgiveness,
For the punishment that's due.

Cleanse their souls, remit their debt,
Let them kneel before Your throne,
So, they may praise and worship in
The glory of Your home."

In the middle of Montana
Off a dirt road on a hill,
Stands a graveyard so forgotten,
Where the dead are sleeping still.

Prayers for the Dying, Prayers for the Dead

Again, it seemed a rainy day had led me to a dream,
My rosary wrapped around my hand and coffee full of cream.
As I settled with a book to read but drifted off to sleep,
I found myself within a fog upon a rocky heap.

It seemed the stones around my feet were used to mark a grave,
And posted as a warning to the entrance of a cave.
I peered into the darkened hole but only saw pitch black,
But then I heard a mournful sound that made me jump straight back.

Such cries, pleas and frightening sounds that made my blood run cold,
I quickly crossed myself and prayed St. Michael's prayer of old.
Suddenly, the air grew still as a light shown in the night,
An Angel beckoned me to kneel and pray with all my might!
"Someone is dying," were his words, "so near the gates of hell."
"Pray hard now for his salvation, before they ring death's bell!"
I threw myself upon the ground, prostrate before the Lord,
And fought for his conversion with my rosary as my sword.

I begged God's Divine Mercy with my arms stretched open wide,
And prayed he'd find repentance and forgiveness as he died.
It seemed I prayed for hours doing battle for his soul,
When lightning struck across the sky and closed that deep dark hole.

Then scores of angels shouted, “Alleluia!” to their King!
As purgatory opened in a mighty rushing swing.
A soul was saved, God’s grace revealed, but no time yet to rest,
A time of expiation due this soul that had been blessed.

Reparation, prayers, and masses now to quench him from the fires,
To see the Holy Face of God, is what the law requires.
So, in charity and kindness, please pray for those who’ve died,
That soon they see the golden gates of heaven open wide.

“For the Souls in purgatory, dear Father, grant release,
So soon their cries are silenced when at last they dwell in peace.
Still, if my dad therein resides, or my grandpa and my aunt,
Please, take them soon to heaven, of this I ask you grant.”

When They Come to Me

They always seem to come to me, just when I fall asleep.
As the darkness overwhelms me, into my mind they seep.
They're the faces of my loved ones, yet some I've never known.
They push and pull into my dreams; some plead, some cry
and moan.

"You have the chance to kiss our Lord,
Each day at Holy Mass.
Yet waste your time on worthless things,
No thoughts your life will pass.

But pass it will, then you'll be judged standing before the Lord.
Condemned for all eternity? Or heaven your reward?
But what if you like us fall short before the Face of God?
Will you like us regret the times your prayer life was so flawed?

Hear us now, and see our pain. Please pray for our release.
Then we in turn shall pray for you your love of God increase.
Waste not your time, for it grows short, but sacrifice and pray!
We ask for your indulgence to reduce our debt away."

With that they usually disappear,
As I kneel in silent prayer,
That soon they see the Face of God,
With no more debt to bear.

Purgatory and Roadside Crosses

My dad is gone, and mom is gone.
My siblings all are too.
There's no one left to pray for me
That's why I'm asking you.
"Is Purgatory real?" you ask.
I can assure you this,
The pain which I am feeling here,
You're going to want to miss!"

On our many travels back and forth between Oklahoma and Montana we have seen many roadside crosses. I am not exaggerating when I say we have seen hundreds of them. On Highway 191 alone there are more than ninety crosses between Bozeman and West Yellowstone, Montana. These memorials are dedicated to persons who have died on those spots on the road in some kind of tragic accident.

Just last Sunday, while returning from Mass, we passed four white crosses along the highway decorated with fresh flowers, obviously representing the deaths of four people. My husband Joel and I began musing about who could have died, and our thoughts were heavy with whether it had been teenagers or a family of four who had perished. The one big question that loomed in both our minds was if they had been prepared to die and ready to meet Almighty God. Also, we thought that if they were now in "Purgatory" would they have anyone here on earth who would pray for them. We both made the Sign of the Cross for the four deceased persons as a quick prayer for them, but then continued on our way up the highway only to find crosses and faded ragged flowers for five more deaths. We made the Sign of the Cross again and both of us let out a sigh of sadness. These crosses were old and broken down just like the faded artificial flowers that adorned them. Time had passed, funerals were over, and the raw, emotional wounds of losing someone had faded as well. Did anyone still think of them? Did anyone still pray for them? Did anyone even know that they *should be praying for someone who had died* in case they needed relief from the pains of purgatory?

What is PURGATORY?

The Catechism of the Catholic Church says:

1030

All who die in God's grace and friendship, but still imperfectly purified, are indeed assured of their eternal salvation; but after death they undergo purification, so as to achieve the holiness necessary to enter the joy of heaven.

1031

The Church gives the name Purgatory to this final purification of the elect, which is entirely different from the punishment of the damned. The Church formulated her doctrine of faith on Purgatory especially at the Councils of Florence and Trent. The tradition of the Church, by reference to certain texts of Scripture, speaks of a cleansing fire:

> As for certain lesser faults, we must believe that, the Final Judgment, there is a purifying fire. He who is truth says that Whoever utters blasphemy against the Holy Spirit will be pardoned neither in this age nor in the age to come. From this sentence we understand that certain offenses can be forgiven in this age, but certain others in the age to come. (End of reference from the Catechism)

One Catholic mom, a close friend of ours, summed it up beautifully, "Punishment in Purgatory is an act of love on the part of the Father to allow us the time to cleanse ourselves of any sin or residue of sin left remaining due to imperfect contrition in our hearts and wills. The majesty and love of God is so holy, divine and profound that unless we are made perfect in our love for Him, we will not allow ourselves to come into His presence but would hurl ourselves out of His presence. (Thus, hurling ourselves into hell.) So, Purgatory becomes a gift of God's grace and love to us that enables us to approach His throne pure, spotless, and clothed in the garments of Christ, making us holy and wholly acceptable to the Father." Well said, dear friend!

My mother has a simpler take on an explanation. While I was growing up, she used to say, "Anyone who dies and does not go to heaven, goes to either purgatory or hell. If they are in hell, we cannot help them. But if they are in purgatory, then they need our prayers. They need our acts of charity through the offering up of our aches, pains, and crosses as reparation for their past forgiven sins. They, (the Poor Souls in purgatory) cannot make amends for themselves, so they rely on us. *Never* forget to pray for them!"

You have got to love Mom's straight to the point explanation!

Pope Leo XIII in his Quod Anniversarius said:

> "Therefore, since it is certain by the doctrine of the Catholic Church, that the souls detained in purgatory are benefited by the prayers of the faithful, and especially by the August sacrifice of the altar, we think we can give them no more useful and desirable pledge of our love than by everywhere increasing the offering of the pure oblation of the Most Holy Sacrifice of our Divine Mediator, for the extinction of their pain.
>
> We therefore decree, with all the necessary dispensations and indulgences, the last Sunday of next September as a day of ample expiation on which will be celebrated by ourselves, and equally by each of our brethren the Patriarchs, Archbishops, and Bishops, and also by other prelates exercising jurisdiction in a diocese, each in his own church, whether patriarchal, metropolitan, or cathedral, a special Mass for the Dead with the greatest solemnity possible, and according to the rite ordered in the Missal for the Commemoration of all Souls."

Having a Mass or Masses said for a deceased loved one is the greatest gift one could ever give! Just ask a priest, and he will be more than happy to say one. Also, a Gregorian Mass series is the celebration of the Holy Sacrifice of the Mass *FOR ONE OF THE DECEASED FAITHFUL* for thirty consecutive days. The Gregorian Mass series is a custom recognized, approved, and encouraged by the Roman Catholic Church. It was born from the practice of the faithful who desired to imitate the charity of Pope Saint Gregory the Great in favor of the monk, Justus, whom the Pope delivered in 590, from the fire of purgatory, by having celebrated for him the Eucharistic Sacrifice during thirty consecutive days. This is quite a commitment for a parish Priest to undertake, so personally, we contact monasteries that have several Priests who may do the Gregorian Masses.

It is by our prayers, our rosaries, or having the Holy Sacrifice of the Mass said, that we can relieve a soul from the pains in purgatory or quite possibly help to free their souls to go to heaven today! We can only imagine the gratitude that they would have for us, and we can be assured of their prayers for both our physical and spiritual needs. Just think, maybe a simple act of kindness, such as bending down to pick up a piece of paper from the floor, offered as a small sacrifice in reparation to our Lord for a soul in purgatory, may be all it takes to get someone out.

What if the saying of the single prayer, "Jesus, Mary, and Joseph, I love you, save souls!" was all it took to relieve or release our grandpas or grandmas from the purifying fires of Purgatory?

Jesus, Mary, and Joseph, I love you, save souls!

Having a Mass said for the dead is the absolute highest means of affording relief to the dead and quite possibly gaining their release from purgatory.

Eternal rest grant unto them, O Lord, and may perpetual light shine upon them. And may their souls, and the souls of all the Faithful departed, through the mercy of God, rest in peace. Amen.

"We have loved him/her in life, let us not abandon him/her until we have conducted him/her by our prayers into the house of the Lord."

O gentlest Heart of Jesus, ever present in the Blessed Sacrament, ever consumed with burning love for the poor captive souls in purgatory,] have mercy on the soul of Thy servant, N.

Bring him/her from the shadows of exile to the bright home in heaven, where, we trust Thou and Thy Blessed Mother, have woven for him/her a crown of unfading bliss.
Amen.

Sweet Heart of Jesus, be my love.

Sweet Heart of Mary, be my salvation.

Merciful Jesus, grant him/her eternal rest.

Bobby and Dorothy

A Sacrament
September 7th, 1947

Dorothy

Dear Blessed Mother, hear me, please,
The words that I now say,
If my Bobby's not in heaven,
Please, take him there today.

Traditional Prayers

for the

Poor Souls in Purgatory

Litany for the Poor Souls in Purgatory

O Jesus, Thou suffered and died that all mankind might be saved and brought to eternal happiness. Hear our pleas for further mercy on the souls of:

My dear parents and grandparents, *my Jesus mercy.*
My brothers and sisters and other near relatives, *my Jesus mercy.*
My godparents and sponsors of Confirmation, *my Jesus mercy.*
My spiritual and temporal benefactors, *my Jesus mercy.*
My friends and neighbors, *my Jesus mercy.*
All for whom love or duty bids me pray, *my Jesus mercy.*
Those who have suffered disadvantage or harm through me, *my Jesus mercy.*
Those who have offended me, *my Jesus mercy.*
Those whose release is near at hand, *my Jesus mercy.*
Those who desire most to be united to Thee, *my Jesus mercy.*
Those who endure the greatest sufferings, *my Jesus mercy.*
Those whose release is most remote, *my Jesus mercy.*
Those who are least remembered, *my Jesus mercy.*
Those who are most deserving on account of their services to the Church, *my Jesus mercy.*
The rich, who are now the most destitute, *my Jesus mercy.*
The mighty, who are now powerless, *my Jesus mercy.*
The once spiritually blind, who now see their folly, *my Jesus mercy.*
The frivolous, who spent their time in idleness, *my Jesus mercy.*
The poor who did not seek the treasures of heaven, *my Jesus mercy.*
The tepid who devoted little time to prayer, *my Jesus mercy.*
The indolent who neglected to perform good works, *my Jesus mercy.*
Those of little faith, who neglected the frequent reception of the Sacraments, *my Jesus mercy.*
The habitual sinners, who owe their salvation to a miracle of grace, *my Jesus mercy.*
Parents who failed to watch over their children, *my Jesus mercy.*
Superiors who were not solicitous for the salvation of those entrusted to them, *my Jesus mercy.*

The worldly minded, who failed to use their wealth and talent for the service of God, *my Jesus mercy.*
Those who witnessed the death of others, but would not think of their own, *my Jesus mercy.*
Those who did not provide for the life hereafter, *my Jesus mercy.*
Those whose sentence is severe because of the great things entrusted to them, *my Jesus mercy.*
The popes, kings, and rulers, *my Jesus mercy.*
The bishops and their counselors, *my Jesus mercy.*
My teachers and spiritual advisors, *my Jesus mercy.*
The priests and religious of the Catholic Church, *my Jesus mercy.*
The defenders of the Holy Faith, *my Jesus mercy.*
Those who died on the battlefield, *my Jesus mercy.*
Those who fought for their country, *my Jesus mercy.*
Those who were buried in the sea, *my Jesus mercy.*
Those who died of apoplexy, *my Jesus mercy.*
Those who died of heart attacks, *my Jesus mercy.*
Those who suffered and died of cancer, *my Jesus mercy.*
Those who died suddenly in accidents, *my Jesus mercy.*
Those who died without the last rites of the Church, *my Jesus mercy.*
Those who shall die within the next twenty-four hours, *my Jesus mercy.*
My own poor soul when I shall have to appear before Thy judgment seat, *my Jesus mercy.*

PRAYER

Eternal rest grant unto them, O Lord, and let perpetual light shine upon them for evermore with Thy Saints, because Thou art gracious. May the prayer of Thy suppliant people, we beseech Thee, O Lord, benefit the souls of Thy departed servants and handmaids: that Thou mayest both deliver them from all their sins, and make them to be partakers of Thy redemption. Amen.

Eternal rest grant unto them, O Lord. And let perpetual light shine on them. Amen.

May their souls and the souls of all the faithful departed through the mercy of God, rest in peace. Amen.

Prayers for the Poor Souls
in
Purgatory
(from the Raccolta)

Most loving Jesus, I humbly beseech Thee, that Thou Thyself wouldst offer to Thine Eternal Father in behalf of the Holy Souls in Purgatory, the Most Precious Blood which poured forth from the sacred wounds of Thine adorable Body, together with Thine agony and death. And do thou likewise, O Sorrowful Virgin Mary, present unto Him together with the dolorous Passion of thy dear Son, thine own sighs and tears, and all the sorrows thou didst suffer in His suffering, in order that, through the merits of the same, refreshment may be granted to the souls now suffering in the fiery torments of purgatory, so that, being delivered from that painful prison, they may be clothed with glory in heaven, there to sing the mercies of God forever and ever. Amen.

Absolve, O Lord, the souls of all the faithful departed from every bond of sin, that with Thy gracious assistance they may deserve to escape the judgment of vengeance and enjoy the blessedness of everlasting light.

V. Eternal rest give unto them, O Lord.
R. And let perpetual light shine upon them.
V. From the gates of hell,
R. Deliver their souls, O Lord.
V. May they rest in peace.
R. Amen.
V. O Lord, hear my prayer.
R. And let my cry come unto Thee.

Let us pray.

O God, the Creator and Redeemer of all the faithful; grant unto the souls of Thy departed servants and handmaids the remission of all their sins: that through our devout supplications they may obtain

the pardon they have always desired. Who livest and reignest world without end. Amen.
My Jesus, by the sorrows Thou didst suffer in Thine agony in the Garden, in Thy scourging and crowning with thorns, in Thy way to Calvary, in Thy crucifixion and death, have mercy on the souls in purgatory, and especially on those that are most forsaken; do Thou deliver them from the dire torments they endure; call them and admit them to Thy most sweet embrace in paradise.

Pray one Our Father, Hail Mary, Eternal rest, etc.

Prayers for Our Parents

O God, who has commanded us to honor our father and our mother; in Thy mercy have pity on the soul of my father (or mother) and forgive him (her) trespasses and make me to see him (her) again in the joy of everlasting brightness. Through Christ our Lord. Amen.
(Roman Missal)

For the Souls in Purgatory

O most gentle Heart of Jesus, ever present in the Blessed Sacrament, ever consumed with burning love for the poor captive souls in purgatory, have mercy on the souls of Thy departed servants. Be not severe in Thy judgments, but let some drops of Thy Precious Blood fall upon the devouring flames. And do Thou, O merciful Savior, send Thy holy angels to conduct them to a place of refreshment, light and peace. Amen.

Our family lost a member,
A mother lost her son,
And brothers once together,
Found they were missing one.

Rest in peace, Cliff.

Chaplet

of the

Poor Souls in Purgatory

(Pray this Chaplet using your Rosary)

Begin with: The Creed on the Crucifix, then one Our Father, three Hail Marys, and the Glory Be on the next five beads for the intentions of the Pope.

On the 'large' beads pray:

O holy souls, draw the fire of God's love into my soul to reveal Jesus crucified in me here on earth, rather than hereafter in purgatory.

On the 'small' beads pray:

Crucified Lord Jesus, have mercy on the souls in purgatory.

Chaplet ends by praying the Glory Be three times.

A plenary indulgence is granted to the Christian faithful who devoutly take part in the adoration of the Cross during the solemn liturgy of Good Friday

A Week of Prayers for the Poor Souls

Every Day Prayer for the Poor Souls

O Lord, hear my prayer.
And let my cry come unto Thee.

O God, the Creator and Redeemer of all the faithful; grant unto the souls of Thy servants and handmaids the remission of all their sins; that through our devout supplications they may obtain the pardon they have always desired. Who livest and reignest world without end. Amen.

Eternal Rest grant unto them and let perpetual light shine upon them. May they rest in peace.

Sunday

O Lord God omnipotent, I beseech Thee by the Precious Blood, which Thy Divine Son Jesus shed in the Garden, deliver the souls in purgatory, and especially that one which is the most forsaken of all, bring it into Thy glory, where it may praise and bless Thee forever. Amen

(Our Father, Hail Mary, Glory Be, Eternal Rest grant unto them and let perpetual light shine upon them. May they rest in peace)

Monday

O Lord God omnipotent, I beseech Thee by the Precious Blood, which Thy Divine Son Jesus shed in His cruel scourging, deliver the souls in purgatory, and among them all, especially that soul which is nearest to its entrance into Thy glory, that it may soon begin to praise Thee and bless Thee forever. Amen.

(Our Father, Hail Mary, Glory Be, Eternal Rest grant unto them and let perpetual light shine upon them. May they rest in peace)

Tuesday

O Lord God omnipotent, I beseech Thee by the Precious Blood which Thy Divine Son Jesus shed in His bitter crowning with thorns, deliver the souls in purgatory, and among them all, particularly that soul which is in the greatest need of our prayers, in order that it may not long be delayed in praising Thee in Thy glory and blessing Thee forever. Amen.

(Our Father, Hail Mary, Glory Be, Eternal Rest grant unto them and let perpetual light shine upon them. May they rest in peace)

Wednesday

O Lord God omnipotent, I beseech Thee by the Precious Blood which Thy Divine Son Jesus shed in the streets of Jerusalem whilst He carried on His sacred shoulders the heavy burden of the Cross, deliver the souls in purgatory and especially that one which is richest in merits in Thy sight, so that, having soon attained the high place in glory to which it is destined, it may praise Thee triumphantly and bless Thee forever. Amen.

(Our Father, Hail Mary, Glory Be, Eternal Rest grant unto them and let perpetual light shine upon them. May they rest in peace)

Thursday

O Lord God omnipotent, I beseech Thee by the Precious Body and Blood of Thy Divine Son Jesus, which He Himself on the night before His passion gave as meat and drink to His beloved Apostles and bequeathed to His holy Church to be the perpetual Sacrifice and life-giving nourishment of His faithful people, deliver the souls in purgatory, but most of all, that soul which was most devoted to the Mystery of Infinite Love, in order that it may praise Thee therefore, together with Thy divine Son and the Holy Spirit in Thy glory forever. Amen

(Our Father, Hail Mary, Glory Be, Eternal Rest grant unto them and let perpetual light shine upon them. May they rest in peace)

Friday

O Lord God omnipotent, I beseech Thee by the Precious Blood which Thy Divine Son Jesus did shed this day upon the tree of the Cross, especially from His sacred hands and feet, deliver the souls in purgatory, and particularly the souls for whom I am most bound to pray, in order that I may not be the cause which hinders Thee from admitting it quickly to the possession of Thy glory where it may praise Thee and bless Thee forevermore. Amen.

(Our Father, Hail Mary, Glory Be, Eternal Rest grant unto them and let perpetual light shine upon them. May they rest in peace)

Saturday

O Lord God omnipotent, I beseech Thee by the Precious Blood, which gushed forth from the sacred Side of Thy Divine Son Jesus in the presence and to the great sorrow of His most holy Mother, deliver the souls in purgatory, and among them all, especially that soul which has been most devout to this noble Lady, that it may come quickly into Thy glory, there to praise Thee in her, and her in Thee through all the ages. Amen.

(Our Father, Hail Mary, Glory Be, Eternal Rest grant unto them and let perpetual light shine upon them. May they rest in peace)

SEQUENCE

Dies irae, dies illa

Day of wrath and doom impending,
David's word with Sibyl's blending,
Heaven and earth in ashes ending!

O what fear man's bosom rendeth,
When from heaven the Judge descendeth,
On whose sentence all dependeth!

Wondrous sound the trumpet flingeth,
Through earth's sepulchers it ringeth,
All before the throne it bringeth.

Death is struck, and nature quaking,
All creation is awaking,
To its Judge an answer making.

Lo! The book exactly worded,
Wherein all hath been recorded;
Thence shall judgment be awarded.

When the judge His seat attaineth,
And each hidden deed arraigneth,
Nothing unavenged remaineth.

What shall I, frail man, be pleading?
Who for me be interceding,
When the just are mercy needing?

King of majesty tremendous,
Who dost free salvation send us,
Found of pity, then befriend us!

Think, kind Jesu – my salvation
Caused Thy Wondrous Incarnation;
Leave me not to reprobation.

Faint and weary Thou hast sought me,
On the Cross of suffering bought me;
Shall such grace be vainly brought me?

Righteous Judge! For sin's pollution
Grant Thy gift of absolution,
Ere that day of retribution.

Guilty, now I pour my moaning,
All my shame with anguish owning;
Spare, O God, thy suppliant groaning!

Through the sinful woman shriven,
Through the dying thief forgiven,
Thou to me a hope hast given.

Worthless are my prayers and sighing,
Yet, good Lord, in grace complying,
Rescue me from fires undying.

With Thy sheep a place provide me,
From the goats afar divide me,
To Thy right hand do Thou guide me.

When the wicked are confounded,
Doomed to shame and woe unbounded,
Call me, with Thy Saints surrounded.

Low I kneel, with heart's submission,
See, like ashes my contrition!
Help me in my last condition!

Ah! That day of tears and mourning!
From the dust of earth returning,
Man for judgment must prepare him:

Spare, O God, in mercy spare him!
Lord, all -pitying, Jesus blest,
Grant them Thine eternal rest.
Amen.

OUT OF THE DEPTHS

De profundis

Out of the depths I cry to You, O Lord:
Lord, hear my voice.
Let Thy ears be attentive
to the voice of my supplication. If Thou, O Lord, wilt mark
iniquities: Lord, who shall stand it. For with Thee
there is merciful forgiveness: and by reason of Thy law, I have waited
for Thee, O Lord. My soul hath relied on His word:
My soul hath hoped in the Lord.
From the morning watch even until night, let Israel hope in the
Lord. Because with the Lord there is mercy: and with Him plentiful
redemption. And He shall redeem Israel from all His iniquities.

Novena for the Holy Souls in Purgatory

(Daniel A. Lord, S.J. 1888-1955)

FIRST DAY

Sin is the one thing that holds back the progress of men and women. True progress is man's ascent to God. Only sin blocks his path. Vice and crime throw human beings back to animal levels when they should be mounting toward the angels.

Death in mortal sin means the complete failure that is hell. It flings a man, who is destined for eternal happiness, into eternal loss and pain. Death in venial sin or with the punishment due to sin still on the soul means a halt in the progress toward heaven. The poor soul – poor indeed in his eagerness to reach God and the tedious, painful delay that keeps him from God – must linger in God's prison-house.

This is the sad land of purgatory. It is a place of anxious, almost impatient waiting.

Since there are in purgatory relatives we loved and friends we knew and thousands of other who call to us for help, we pause and say:

DAILY PRAYER FOR THE HOLY SOULS

O God, the creator and redeemer of all the faith, grant to the souls of Thy servants and handmaids departed, the remission of all their sins; that through pious supplications they may obtain the pardon they have always desired. Who livest and reignest with God the Father in the unity of the Holy Ghost, God, world without end. Amen.

SECOND DAY

Nothing else is humanly harder to bear than painful waiting.

All the souls in purgatory are sure one day to reach heaven. They know how wonderful heaven is and how desirable is God. But they cannot follow the violent impulse that drives them toward their happiness. They must hunger for God and still be withheld from the possession of Him. In hell there is only bleak and hopeless despair.

In purgatory there is hope and certainty and love and eagerness – and long periods of waiting...waiting...waiting...

There is suffering too in purgatory, the suffering that washes away, in flame the stains of guilt and cleanses as with fire the soul that will eventually enter into the presence of the spotless God. But the real pain of purgatory is that awful eagerness for God who is just out of reach, and that longing to go home to heaven, which is almost seen but as yet unattainable.

Nothing defiled can enter heaven; that we know. So, purgatory is the place where defilement is removed, where the souls that are destined for glory are prepared by punishment and tedious delay for their glorious home-coming with God.

For the love we bear our friends in purgatory we pray:

Recite "The Prayer for the Holy Souls."

THIRD DAY

This life on earth is, as we have heard a thousand times, a time of merit. When through the Church's indulgences we avail ourselves of the merits of Christ and of the saints, we can wipe away the guilt of forgiven sins and eliminate the punishment due to venial sins, as we can also do through penance and deeds of charity.

But once the soul enters purgatory, the time for that soul to gain merit is ended. When we suffer on earth, we can offer our suffering to God, increasing thereby our future happiness in heaven and cancelling out the pains of purgatory. When a soul suffers in purgatory, he slowly and tediously cancels the debts of sins; he gains no further merit for heaven. Nor are there indulgences in purgatory, nor fresh use of the merits of Christ, of His Mother, and of the saints.

Thanks however to our union in the Mystical Body of Christ, thanks to the communion of the saints, we can gain merit for the suffering souls. We can win indulgences and apply them to the period of waiting of these souls. We can cut their sufferings and speed their entry into heaven by whatever of good that we offer for them on earth.

In all generosity we say for these souls who depend upon us:

Recite "The Prayer for the Holy Souls".

FOURTH DAY

Swiftly the memory even of the dear dead seems to pass from human minds. Memory is like the tears upon a coffin, swiftly evaporated, quickly dried. The rush of the days fills the minds and the hands of the living. The press of old associations and the establishment of new friends helps supplant and elbow into the dusty corners of our minds the friends now hidden in God's penitentiary.

But these prisoners do not forget us.

In the slow, painful dragging of the days they have time to remember. They are so hungry for God that they have little heart for new companions. They are made sensitive – as pain always makes us sensitive – to memory, to neglect, to hope for deliverance, to the knowledge that those who once cried aloud their love have so swiftly forgotten. With gratitude do they think of those who do remember them. With sadness they think of those who have so swiftly dropped them.

They pray to God, who loves them even in their exile, for the thoughtful and the mindful. They beg that those who have pushed them away for the near and the living will drop into their prison house a thought, a prayer, a good deed in ransom. Remembering our own dear dead, we pray for them:

Recite "The Prayer for the Holy Souls".

FIFTH DAY

These in purgatory are the friends of God. These are the souls who will in a short time be glorious and powerful saints in heaven. Their souls are saved. Their crowns are awaiting them. Their thrones are prepared, and their mansions are ready. God loves them deeply, as He loves all those faithful sons and daughters who fought the good fight. Their prayers for others come straight to His throne. They can no longer pray for themselves; their time to merit is over. They can pray, and they do pray for those on earth whom they love.

That loving mother in purgatory is interceding for her children. That devoted father is now more devoted, and those friends have not forgotten the value of their friendship. Those relatives are bound to us with ties much closer than blood. Most of all, the holy souls pray for their benefactors. Our slight remembering of them wins for us a great measure of intercession from them. We pray thoughtlessly; they pray with the intensity of souls who are coming ever closer to God. We ask for deliverance for them; they beg God for a thousand blessings for us. In sheer wisdom and to our own advantage we say:

Recite "The Prayer for the Holy Souls".

SIXTH DAY

Our souls hunger for God with far more intensity than ever a starving body hungers for food. Here in this world we are distracted by the pressure of the life about us. In purgatory there are no distractions. Their eyes fixed on the closed gates of heaven, the holy souls long for God, yearn for God, hunger and thirst for God. The terms of their sentence ring in their ears: "Thus and thus long shall you remain separated from your joy, until these sins and these misdeeds and these blemishes and these stains have been atoned for."

Balanced against their consuming hunger for God is their certainty that they would not dare enter His presence with the slightest stain upon them. They almost wish that the fires burned more fiercely and more rapidly so that the pain could be at once more intense and more cleansing.

Imagine then their gratitude for every prayer or good deed by which we help them cleanse their souls and speed them on their way to God. Imagine the leaping joy with which they welcome any act by which we cut their sentence, shorten their stay in purgatory, and hasten their entrance into heaven. We can give joy to these holy souls here and now as we say:

Recite "The Prayer for the Holy Souls".

SEVENTH DAY

What food is to a starving man...

What drink is to the parched sailor riding the tropic seas on a raft...

What light is to the man long blind...

What restored health is to the patient invalid...

What freedom is to the prisoner...

All this and far, far more is release from purgatory to a holy soul. And when food, light, health, and freedom come suddenly, unexpectedly, the human heart leaps and bounds, and the soul knows the sharp ecstasy of joy. So, it is with each prayer that we say for the beseeching souls in purgatory. Our prayer is bread and water and light and health; it is a reprieve and a release and freedom and a home-coming. It is the cutting of bonds, the lessening of weary waiting, the termination of exile, the sudden glorious lift that picks them up and seems almost to shoot them toward the center of their joy, God Himself.

For us that prayer is an almost careless gesture. For us a routine act of charity. Prayer, alms, a bit of fasting, a good deed done – forgotten in the doing. For them something beyond price and measure, something for which they can repay us only in the immortal coin of eternity.

Such a good deed we perform as we pray:

Recite "The Prayer for the Holy Souls".

EIGHTH DAY

Then on a happy day release comes.

Perhaps for souls whose friends on earth forgot them and for whom because of valid reasons God showed not special consideration that release comes only at the end of long and bitter centuries. Perhaps it comes far sooner than they dared to hope. Their friends have remembered them. Prayers have poured in upon them. God has accepted these in part or in full payment of their debt.

But late or soon the release comes, the sentence is finished, the grim gates of purgatory swing open. Ahead are the white and shining portals of the eternal city. Like the rush of light, the released soul sweeps upward toward God. Fierce winds have not the fierce intensity that marks this flight of a soul from exile to the happiness for which God destined it. Then in the presence of God there is the moment of triumph, the welcome by the Trinity, the entrance into the heavenly mansion ... the enthronement of another saint. As that moment shall begin for that soul, an eternity of bliss and incomparable happiness that shall be without flaw, never to be marred by uncertainty or disillusionment. For then, the soul shall possess God for all eternity.

We can have part in that swift flight to joy if we pray:

Recite "The Prayer for the Holy Souls".

NINTH DAY Joy does not cause the souls in heaven to forget. On the contrary joy makes them more alive to memory. The soul that has entered into bliss does not for a second forget the generous friends on earth who helped him reach God and glory. Now a saint in heaven, he uses to the full extent his power of intercession. He prays God to be merciful and generous to the generous. By name he mentions to Christ and to Mary those who mentioned his name when he was helpless to help himself. He speaks to the Trinity about his friends. He becomes in effect a mighty benefactor, persuasively beseeching God to extend mercy and grant favors to those who remembered him in purgatory.

He prays with the fervor of new-found joy that their passage through life will be safe, their stay in purgatory brief, their entrance into heaven swift and triumphant. He prays that one day they too might behold the beatific vision and see God, face to face through the endlessness of eternity. It is their unselfish urge to share so great a bliss that we ask them to send us.

To help insure for ourselves a shortened purgatory, we pray:

Recite "The Prayer for the Holy Souls".

A Prayer to St. Joseph for a Soul in Purgatory

Great Saint Joseph, who hast so tenderly loved Jesus and felt so keenly the loss of His Presence during the time that thou was in Limbo, I earnestly recommend to thee the soul of (mention name), who may at this moment be suffering in Purgatory. Be thou his consoler in that place of suffering and expiation! Deign to apply to him the pious suffrages of the faithful, particularly my own; be thou his intercessor with Jesus and Mary and obtain by thy prayers that, delivered from the bonds that hold him in captivity, he may fly to the bosom of God, there to be eternally in the enjoyment of those delights with which the elect are blessed. Amen.

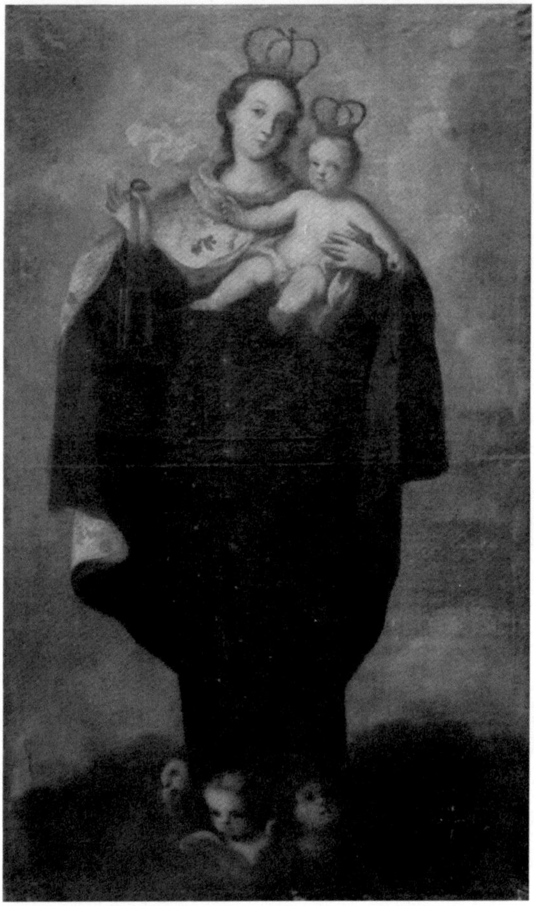

Our Lady of Mount Carmel Brown Scapular and the Sabbatine Privilege

In 1251, our Lady gave to St. Simon Stock a scapular for the Carmelite order along with the following promise: "Take this Scapular, it shall be a sign of salvation, a protection in danger and a pledge of peace. Whosoever dies wearing this Scapular shall not suffer eternal fire." She further says: "Wear it devoutly and perseveringly. It is my garment. To be clothed in it means you are continually thinking of me, and I in turn, am always thinking of you and helping you to secure eternal life."

Another important aspect of wearing the Scapular is the Sabbatine Privilege. This concerns a promise made by Our Lady to Pope John XXII. In a papal letter he issued, he recounted a vision that he had. He stated that the Blessed Virgin told him that those who persevere in wearing the Brown Scapular would receive the grace of going to heaven. "I, the Mother of Grace, shall descend on the Saturday after their death, and whomsoever I shall find in Purgatory, I shall free, so that I may lead them to the holy mountain of life everlasting."

There are three requirements to make oneself eligible for this privilege: 1st, they must wear the Brown Scapular of Carmel; 2nd, they must observe chastity according to their state of life; 3rd, recite the Little Office of Our Blessed Mother (The Rosary can be substituted for the office by obtaining permission from a priest.)
To obtain the fullest possible benefits from the Brown Scapular devotion, one must be validly invested (sometimes called enrolled) in the Brown Scapular by a priest. Every priest has the privilege of enrolling Catholics in the Scapular. After having received the initial blessed Scapular from a priest, no other Brown Scapular need be blessed before wearing. The blessing and imposition are attached to the wearer for life.

Our Lady of Mount Carmel, pray for us now and at the hour of our death. Amen.

Works Cited

Front Cover photo of maternal great-grandparents of the author, Thomas and Margaret Stander.

Photo of the Stander family of Oklahoma City, Oklahoma. Late 1940's

Cabrera, Miguel. (1695-1768). *St. Gertrude.* Dallas Museum of Art. Oil on Canvas. https://www.dma.org/collection/artwork/miguel-cabrera/saint-gertrude-santa-gertrudis

Mountain View Cemetery. Billings, Montana.

Roadside message, Montana

Jackson Joseph Robinson, author's grandson.

Rest in peace, Bobby Leehan, author's father.

Young Blood Cemetery, Panola County, Texas.

Kent Cemetery, Montana

 Maternal grandparents of the author, George and Lorene Stander.

 Highway 191, Gallatin Valley, Montana.

Alexander and Ruth Colbert, known as Pokini and Mofo, favorite names for the parents of friends of the author. They were proud of their Choctaw heritage. Rest in peace.

Bobby and Dorothy Leehan, parents of the author.

Dorothy Leehan.

George and Lorene Stander, rest in peace.

Mike and Oma Francka wedding. Aunt of the author, with her parents, George and Lorene Stander, and his parents, Mike and Ann Francka.

Clifford Wayne Foster, cousin of the author. Requeiscat in pace.

Romero, Lorenzo. ca. *Our Lady of Carmel.* ca. 1740-1750. El Paso Museum of Art. https://commons.wikimedia.org/wiki/File:%27Our_Lady_of_Carmel%27_by_Lorenzo_Romero,_El_Paso_Museum_of_Art.JPG

Giaquinto, Corrado. *The Trinity with Souls in Purgatory.* Early 1740s. Minneapolis Institute of Arts. Public Domain https://commons.wikimedia.org/wiki/File:Corrado_Giaquinto

Back cover photo of fraternal great-grandparents of the author. Jeremiah Robert and Bridget Anne Folan Leehan.

Other Books by the Author

The Seven Sorrows of the Blessed Virgin Mary
Poems in Honor of Our Lady of Sorrows

About the Author

Born and raised in central Oklahoma, USA, Donna Sue Berry is a wife, mother of two, and grandmother of twelve. She and retired rancher husband, Joel Doc, share their time between the wheat fields of Oklahoma and the mountains of Montana. Donna Sue began writing poetry and song lyrics soon after she first read Romeo and Juliet during her junior year in high school. However, it wasn't until she enrolled in her freshman year at the University of Central Oklahoma (at age 47) that her poetry began to deepen and truly express her great love for her Catholic faith. Her favorite poems are rhyming, story poems which weave around a person's thoughts and emotions. She says she writes with an Oklahoman's heart and accent.

The Holy Trinity with Souls in Purgatory

25208074R00038

Made in the USA
San Bernardino, CA
09 February 2019